How to Talk
So Men Will Listen

Also by Marian K. Woodall

Thinking on Your Feet—softcover
Thinking on Your Feet—audiocassette
Speaking to a Group—softcover

How to Talk So Men Will Listen

Marian K. Woodall

PBC
PROFESSIONAL BUSINESS COMMUNICATIONS

Lake Oswego, Oregon 97035

HOW TO TALK SO MEN WILL LISTEN

Grateful acknowledgement is made for permission to reprint excerpts from the following:

Cooper, Morton, Change Your Voice, *Change Your Life*, Macmillan Publishing Company, New York, 1985.
Frank, Milo O., *How to Get Your Point Across in 30 Seconds*, Simon & Schuster, Inc., New York, 1986.
LeRoux, Paul, *Selling to a Group*, Harper & Row, Publishers, Inc., New York, 1984.
Tannen, Deborah, *You Just Don't Understand: Women and Men in Conversation*, William Morrow and Company, Inc., New York, 1990.

Printed in the United States of America

Current printing (last digit):
10 9 8 7 6 5 4 3 2 1

Library of Congress Cataloging-in-Publication Data

Woodall, Marian K., 1941–
    How to talk so men will listen / Marian K. Woodall.
      p. cm.
    Includes bibliographical references.
    ISBN 0-941159-25-6 (pbk.) : 7.95
    1. Communication—Psychological aspects. 2. Nonverbal communication. 3. Women—Language. 4. Communication—Sex differences. I. Title.
P96.P75W66 1990
305.3—dc20
                                              90-62322
                                              CIP

Published and Distributed by
Professional Business Communications
11830 S.W. Kerr Parkway, Suite 350
Lake Oswego, Oregon 97035
503-293-1163 — for inquiries
800-447-5911 — for orders

Dedication

To Lorna Vahlberg Biggers,
my first role model,
with great thanks.

Acknowledgements

Thanks are gratefully offered to many people for inspiration, ideas, encouragement, enthusiasm, and material. You each know how you helped:

Institute for Managerial and Professional Women (Portland, OR)

A Woman's Educational and Leadership Forum (Washington, DC)

Friends and family members Kent Franklin, Kay and Parker Woodall, Bill Woodall, Linda and Charles Marshall, Susan Walsh, Sharon Nelsen, Carol Bond, Edith Rydberg, Barbra Franklin.

Professional publishing associates Debra Lindland; Judy Binder; Dennis and Linny Stovall of Blue Heron Publishing/Media Weavers; Michael Pearce, 21st Century Graphics; Jane Loftus; and L.grafix.

Contents

Preface

This is not a sexist book. When I was first approached in 1988 by the Institute for Managerial and Professional Women in Portland, Oregon, to make a presentation on the subject of talking so men would listen, my reaction was lukewarm, to say the least. "That seems like a sexist topic," I said, "but I'll think about it." I put the phone down, and without realizing it, my hand began to move on a piece of paper. It began jotting down ideas, almost in spite of my will. I realized immediately that there were some specific communication suggestions that would help women get people's attention. So I called back and said, "Yes, I'll give a speech called "How to Talk So Men Will Listen." The rest is, as they say, history.

Since that time thousands of people—mostly women—have shared ideas and tips with me in workshops and presentations on this topic across the country. Their insistence about the accuracy of these ideas and the enthusiasm for the tips overwhelmed me. Their expression of need affirmed that these strategies are helpful, even though there will be those who say, as one audience member once responded, that they are "ideas and strategies to perpetuate the old style management 'postures' and 'tricks' that are not working in our management today."

This is not, strictly speaking, a gender book either, though gender often plays a part. There are gender differences in the way people speak. Identifying and understanding these differences are necessary if people wish to change. Since women are the ones who most frequently complain of not being listened to, it is vital that women understand the ways in which they sabotage themselves when trying to get their point across. It is helpful to recognize the speech mannerisms and counterproductive non-verbal communicating women project that result in their being ignored. But it is also dangerous to speak of gender differences. I join with sociolinguist Deborah Tannen, who asserts that "despite the dangers, I am joining the growing dialogue on gender and language because the risk of ignoring is greater than the danger of naming them" (*You Just Don't Understand*, p. 16).

This is also not a scholarly tome. Its intent is not to present all the research that has come out in the last few years on gender-based communications. However, theory and research are woven into this material, and a list of resources appears in the back of the book. One significant reason that research does not play a large part in the book is that the material has been "field-tested" with thousands of listeners and workshop participants. The reactions—from both women and men—have provided a great deal of the credibility and support for these tips and comments.

And this book's purpose is more "how to" than why. For a thorough, yet wonderfully readable discussion of why, run, don't walk, to get Dr. Deborah Tannen's latest book, *You Just Don't Understand: Women and Men in Conversation*. This is the full scholarly treatment of male-female conversation styles, yet its sociolinguistic approach is enhanced with examples and anecdotes in which you will surely see yourself.

Support comes also from my 30 years' experience as a professional speech communicator. Through my work as a professional speech coach, speaker, trainer, consultant and college professor, I have worked with thousands of people who wanted to be stronger managers, better sales reps, more astute customer service people, more proficient secretaries—the list goes on and on. The empirical evidence gleaned from all these people's success is another part of the support which stands behind these ideas for better communicating. In fact, the essential message for getting people to listen is precisely the same message from my first two books, *Thinking on Your Feet* (covering one-to-one communicating) and *Speaking to a Group* (which deals with speaking in front of others). The heart of the message with all three types of audiences is

- consider the perspective of your audience
- get their attention
- put the main point up front
- be brief.

This is a book about change. To get others to react in a different way, you must change. You cannot hope to make them change. They may make some movement as a result of your change, but you cannot and must not count on it. If people are not listening to you, plan to make changes in the way you speak. So this is a how-to book, a practical guide for that change. By changing, you will improve your chances to be heard, to be truly listened to, and to be understood when you speak to others.

This is a book about a special communication situation: getting others to listen when you speak. This special situation requires specific communication skills that you can learn and practice. These skills are more necessary than ever because everyone is so busy there is little time to chat. People need to get information in a way that is both concise and timely.

It is a book about power—ways to become more effective (and thus more powerful) by being listened to, whether you are speaking one to one, to a small group, or in front of a large group. This power—indeed, this need for power—exists for both women and men of all ages. That need represents yet another reason this is neither a gender book nor a sexist book. It is also a book about power because it helps you to get more audience for your ideas. Insofar as the success of an idea is proportional to the number of people who hear it, getting larger audiences enhances your power.

This is also a book about age. As people get older, their need to be listened to grows at about the same rate as younger people's impatience when listening to them. Older people need tools to combat this impatience. If younger people are unwilling to listen to their elders, all the elders can do is make changes in their own approach; they cannot change the young people any more than women can change their mates or employees can change their bosses.

Finally, it is a book about equality. Equality is a key goal for powerless or ineffective people, regardless of gender or age, who hope to get the treatment they want and the attention they need, expect to succeed in getting their ideas across, and expect to be listened to. Insofar as most people need to be respected and taken seriously, it is a book for all of us.

Introduction

You Can Change Only Yourself

This book might well have been titled *How to Talk So Your Boss Will Listen*, or *How to Talk So Your Adult Children Will Listen*, or even simply, *How to Talk So Others Will Listen*. It is a how-to-do-it book, using a communications skills-as-tools approach. If something is not working, we seek tools to make it work.

One thing that is not working well in our busy, complex society is the listening part of our communicating. Failure to listen—to listen accurately—has long been considered by communications experts as the biggest single problem in communications at all levels among all people. We cannot actually get people to listen better; what we can do is speak better so that they are more inclined to listen. There are tools here to improve everyone's ability to speak.

This book's primary focus, however, is on the male-female communicating that most of us are a daily part of, at home, and to a great extent, at work. There is little disagreement that the communications between men and women leave some significant gaps. These are tools to improve some specific gaps. Be aware that they are not tools to solve the intrinsic differences between the communicating styles of men and women—styles that distinguish and frequently divide males and females in their attempt to reach each other.

Do these tools work? They do. These tools require some changes. You must want to make the changes in yourself. Your goal, in fact, must be solely to change yourself. You cannot change anybody else.

Can people change? Can women speak more assertively? Can timid men speak more forcefully? Can older people speak more briefly? Can powerless people change? The answer to all these questions is "Yes, to some extent." The changes are possible only "to some extent" because it is a lifetime of habits and patterns that need to be modified.

It is also "to some extent" possible because these tools are not meant to be a blueprint for reshaping one's entire communicating style. None of us will likely affect every talking opportunity. We must pick our spots.

CHAPTER ONE

Why Won't Anybody Listen to Me?

In a hurry?

• *get to the point*
• *use only a few details*

Board room or breakfast table, you begin to relate something to your boss, a staffer, spouse, or adult child. Midway through the fifth or sixth sentence, you realize he is not giving you his undivided attention. In fact, he is giving you virtually no attention at all: no eye contact, no nods, no softly-voiced reactions. What is your clue that you have no audience? The lack of eye contact and nods should be strong signals; but the most significant clue is within your own consciousness: *your fifth or sixth sentence*. That's right, you talked too long before getting to the point.

Poor communicators tend to talk in paragraphs. Successful communicators—people who want to be listened to, people who command respect—tend to talk in short sentences and even in bulleted items. Surprised? You shouldn't be. When is the last time you delivered a long, detailed explanation? Did you feel that your words were not receiving the attention you wanted? Your response to both those questions is probably from the same situation: one in which you were talking in paragraphs. You probably gave a speech. That is a common problem, especially when people are excited or preoccupied about a cause or idea they are involved with, a project they are working on.

People who do not get listened to tend to talk in unending sentences. Such a person is characterized by the eminent mystery novelist, Ngaio Marsh, in *Artists in Crime*. The woman (for she *is* a woman, alas) is named Lucy Lorrimer. Marsh writes, "She was known never to finish a sentence. She always got lost in the thicket of secondary thoughts that sprang up round her simplest remarks, so everybody used to say, 'as lucid as Lucy Lorrimer.'"

Most of you know someone who talks in unending sentences. They begin to tell you a simple story and then double back to give a little piece of background about a detail, and a little tidbit about that background, and then a little piece of insider information about that tidbit. Sometimes those people actually do remember where they're going and finally get to the point, if we are patient enough to listen. But more often, they get lost in the thicket of secondary thoughts, just as Lucy Lorrimer does.

Here is a sample of the endlessly woven monologue that such people tend to create:

> *Well, I think I finally have an inside track on that job I was hoping to get at the architects' firm. I had lunch with Janice, you remember that she's a member of the arts committee and she and I have worked together on several projects, including the marketing proposal, which took so many meetings. At any rate, she and I went to lunch and we talked about some of the problems that they have. She's concerned, because she's so busy, about being able to get a big enough project planned and developed that her boss would buy into it. I was concerned about not being able to meet her boss, but she felt like she could make the project go okay, so we talked about the project, and when we were coming back from lunch I happened to be turning around on the steps just as a friend of mine, Doug Gillan—he's the director of the arts organization that Janice and I both belong to— came by with Janice's boss. Well, Doug was kind enough to introduce us, and as I talked to Janice's boss, I mentioned an article in Harvard Business Review that I thought was related to the project that Janice and I were talking about, and he, in fact, said that he knew the editor of Harvard Business Review and had hoped that he was getting a complimentary subscription from his friend who was the editor. As we talked, it was clear that he liked me and was tuned into what I was saying and seemed to*

have good eye contact and good non-verbal re-
sponse to me, so I hope that I'll get that job.

The problems with unending sentences and secondary thoughts that constantly double back is obvious: taking too long to get to the point and providing
too many details.

The Problems, the Solutions—Briefly

The major culprits, then, are taking too long to
get to the point and using too many details to expand
that point. What quick solutions exist?

- put your point first
- follow with just the essential details, itemized.

These solutions may seem too simple; yet you
recognize that people are busy. You owe them the
courtesy of clear and precise information or opinions.
That is what you want, too. Try to remember the last
time you sat enthusiastically, or even patiently,
through a long, detailed account of something. Most
people will not listen with all that much patience either.

You first need to get people's attention with the
strength and brevity of your idea. After you have se-
cured their attention, then you can engage them in a
dialogue. As they ask questions and add their input
they become involved. You can add the additional
details as they request them. Note: They seldom want

as many details as you would like to offer, unless you're talking to your best friend from high school.

If you have a problem getting people to listen, you already know it. Decide right now whether that knowledge frets you or disturbs you enough to do something about it.

Jot down names of individuals or situations where a failure to get attention has frustrated you. Assess individually how much each of these people or situations caused you to be unproductive, disgruntled, or simply irritated. Make a commitment now to create some changes in your talking habits.

CHAPTER TWO

It's a Communication Skill

Why is it helpful—even necessary—to read a book about how to get people's attention? Three compelling reasons come immediately to mind:

- it's a special communication situation
- it's a skill
- it's the first stage of a conversation.

Getting people's attention these days has become "a special communication situation." Why? Everyone is busy. People are so distracted by telephones, fax machines, computers, instant everything, they do not have the time to pay attention to others.

As a result, people are less patient with those who have trouble getting to the point, less willing to let people ramble on and on, and unwilling to sift the details to find the message. Therefore, if you wish to get people's attention, you must learn the techniques of a special communication situation.

Getting people to listen is also a *skill*. According to the dictionary, skill is a "proficiency or ability" to accomplish a task. Two facets comprise building a skill: technique and practice. Anyone who has ever experienced frustration—even anger—at not getting the attention they sought for an idea or opinion can learn the skill of talking so others will listen.

Finally, a conversation is the goal. However simplistic it sounds, you need the attention of another person to develop a conversation. It is through conversation that involvement occurs; you need the involvement of your listener to make anything happen.

A Special Communication Situation

Examples of special communication situations include job interviewing, giving a speech, running an effective meeting, telemarketing, closing a sale. These situations all require particular expertise. They require special techniques and practice. You are risking failure if you try to wing it in any of these special situations.

When interviewing candidates for a position in your company, you are not likely to be successful if you simply invite them in and chat with them. Even though the basis of an interview is a question and answer format, just any old questions will not do; a knowledge of question patterns is necessary. It is essential to know how to read a resume to establish a candidate's background before the interview. It is helpful to then prepare appropriate questions to discover the candidate's aptitudes, attitudes, and goals. Though the situation appears to be a conversation, much preparation and knowledge are needed to successfully interview candidates.

Similar kinds of preparation and expertise are required for running effective meetings, giving speeches, telemarketing and closing sales. These, too, are special communication situations in which people must learn techniques and practice them until proficient. Success most often comes from planning and knowledge.

So too, getting people to listen has become a special communication situation. When making a brief report to a committee, requesting new equipment from the boss, asking for an opinion from one's spouse, the old days of winging it are, for the most part, over. People who have listened to my speeches on this topic sometimes moan, "I don't want every conversation with my spouse or my boss or my children to be a 'special communication situation.' Do I have to follow the techniques and skills that we're talking about every single time?" I laugh and respond, "No, only those times when you wish to be listened to." Besides, what you are doing is getting their attention; once you have it, the conversation you seek will likely occur (See below).

A Skill

Getting people to listen is a skill. The word *skill* has precise implications. Skill implies something that can be learned. It implies a set of steps, techniques, and tips, and it especially implies practice. Think about what you do that you are skillful at, whether it is pie-baking, golf, painting, growing roses, or skiing. You got that way by learning some techniques, perhaps taking some lessons, picking up some tips along the way, and practicing. One day, as you were baking your pie crust or shushing down the slope, you thought to yourself, "Hey! I'm good at this." Likewise, getting people to listen can be developed so you will one day say to yourself, "Hey! I'm good at this. People listen to me. People pay attention to me when I speak."

The First Stage of Conversation

Conversation is the goal. Gaining a person's attention is the first stage of building a conversation. Once the connection is made, both individuals add details and talk as fully as they would like, with great likelihood of involvement. (See page 44 for more on conversation building.)

Getting people to pay attention to your ideas, feelings, emotions, reactions, and opinions takes skill. This skill can be developed like any other communication skill. Resolve to develop this skill. Your satisfaction in relationships will be greater; your power will be greater.

CHAPTER THREE

It's a Gender Issue

In a hurry?

• *say less than you want to say*

Let's talk about the men versus women situation right away. To some extent, getting people to listen to you is a gender issue. The empirical evidence (i.e., just look around you) is too strong to suggest otherwise. There is little arguing the point that women have difficulty getting the men in their lives—business, social, and personal—to listen when they talk. Ask any woman.

Deborah Tannen's sociolinguist studies as presented in her new book, *You Just Don't Understand: Woman and Men In Conversation*, clearly indicate that men and women have distinct differences in their communicating styles. Yet, one seldom hears a man complain that his wife or secretary doesn't listen to him. (Why that may be true is another book for Dr. Tannen!) Since it is women who express the problem, this chapter focuses on women's communicating styles.

Studies demonstrate the specific speech manner-isms and communications characteristics that inhibit women's ability to be commanding and forceful. An article titled "Sex Roles, Interruptions and Silences in Conversation" in *Language and Sex* written in 1975, described studies that demonstrated men tend to in-terrupt women with impunity (Zimmerman and West). No other single aspect of one-to-one commu-nication signals more clearly to a woman that what she has to say is not worth listening to and is not be-ing listened to.

The thousands of women (and men) who have crowded the room, sat on the floor, and spilled out into the hall in my workshops from Alaska to Virginia are in overwhelming agreement about the severity of this problem. Cries of "Right on!" come from my speech coaching clients, from members of women's groups, and from brand new secretaries. Agreement concerning the gender aspect of this communication difficulty has come from friends and associates who have significant relationships—even marriages!—ranging from 45 years to a few weeks. So, it is a gender issue.

However, it is also an age issue and a power issue. The same communications traits sabotage the effec-tiveness of almost everyone at times. Most of us are effective in getting the attention of some people, but not others. Older people lament that they seem less successful and less effective with every passing year.

Failure to get attention for our ideas makes those ideas—and us—less powerful. These two issues are discussed in the next two chapters.

How Women Tend to Talk

Women are acknowledged as having great strength in areas of communication that are vital to business (and family) harmony. The communicating skills that foster this strength include listening, consensus building, and facilitation. These characteristics, while essential in group communicating, sometimes work against their goals of being listened to, of being powerful.

Research shows that women's speech also tends to reflect certain communicating characteristics (emphasis here on the word tend, because naturally not all women have these characteristics). Many of these characteristics are positive in the broad scope of communicating activities. Ironically, some of them hinder women's attempts to gain attention when talking. Four categories of communicating characteristics will be helpful to examine:

- consensus-building skills
- non-verbal traits
- speech mannerisms
- communicating tendencies.

Consensus-Building Skills

Women possess many outstanding communications skills. They bring important—even essential—skills to the communications of business and to the business of communicating. Women

- listen well
- ask questions
- facilitate group problem solving
- read non-verbal communications well
- are sensitive to the opinions, reactions, and fears of other individuals or groups.

Listening

Listening is essential. Effective listening is caring listening, because it shows people you are truly concerned with their problems, their concerns, their opinions, their work, and their activities. That is a tremendous strength. Being listened to is a gratifying and essential human need. Everyone needs to be listened to. This skill also enhances women's abilities in reaching consensus, at drawing out participants in a conversation, and at facilitating group process and problem solving. Naturally, listening is a key way these processes occur.

So what is wrong with being a good listener? The downside of this positive communications trait is that, ironically, women are too good at listening. As will be examined below, a woman often is so busy listening that she fails to get out her point of view. She is so busy being a good listener that she forgets to talk.

Ask Questions

Women ask questions. This trait contributes to their abilities to build consensus, because you have to know what others think and feel in order to guide discussions and reach agreement. Like listening, if carried too far, this desirable trait turns against the questioner: She is less likely to get her own opinion out if she is questioning constantly. If her position is contrary to the opinions she has been soliciting, she is even less likely to contribute it. (See below for more on questioning as a trait.)

Facilitating

In business as well as at home there is a time for consensus building. Through their strengths of listening and asking questions, women bring an essential skill to both arenas. But there is also a time for stating, not asking. Women need to recognize that their stating must at times take priority over their facilitating. Women must learn to distinguish between the two needs and to recognize when stating time arrives.

Read Non-Verbal Communications

Popular opinion has long held and research supports the belief that women are more perceptive in reading and responding to the unspoken messages of non-verbal communications. Part of this success accompanies thoughtful listening, because much of what is "heard" are the messages being sent by the eyes, the body language, and the vocal qualities.

Yet when women are talking too much, giving too many details, they are apparently unable—or unwilling—to react to the non-verbal signals that their listeners give: eyes that glaze over, fidgeting, wandering attention, interruptions.

Sensitivity to Feelings

The comments above bear repeating here. Somehow, the ability to "read between the lines" as people speak does not translate to self-awareness when women are speaking to others. Women need to be more sensitive to how people respond when they talk. They need to recognize they are not giving what others want in terms of amount of detail and prioritizing information—in short, that they are not providing information in a way that it can best be dealt with: precise, direct, to the point, and brief.

Non-Verbal Traits

Three non-verbal traits of female communications patterns need additional attention. Women tend to

- allow interruptions
- use an unassertive voice
- have inadequate eye contact.

Allow Interruptions

Allowing interruptions or neglecting to challenge people who interrupt are habits of weak and power-less people. It may be a chicken and egg issue: What came first, the interruptions or the willingness to al-low them? Whatever the answer, this tendency is more of a problem for women, according to studies in which conversations between men and women and between men and men were tape-recorded and stud-ied. One study showed that the interruptions be-tween men and men were balanced between the speakers, but that in the male-female pairs the men interrupted female listening partners 96 percent more often than women interrupted male partners (Zimmerman and West).

Posture, too, plays a role in being perceived as interruptable. A person slumped or hunched over in a chair, rather than sitting tall and confident, begs to be ignored. A woman standing in a submissive pos-ture, with head slightly bowed and wrists crossed in front, looks powerless before she even begins to speak.

The quick solutions to what to do about inter-ruptions are these: 1) Keep talking, but with a firmer, louder voice. Often the interrupter will stop. 2) Stop right where you are, in the middle of a sentence. Wait. 3) Look pointedly at the interrupter, and say in a firm but polite voice, "I'll be happy to continue when you finish," or "when you finish interrupting me."

Some of my female clients express a hesitancy to take the last, firmest route. You should have little fear, because interruptions are rude in nearly all situations, and most everyone knows that.

Finally, although not a reflection of a non-verbal characteristic, consider the person who takes too long to get to the point: she is almost begging to be interrupted.

Use an Unassertive Voice

Women not only allow people to interrupt them; they unfortunately even encourage interruptions, primarily with an unassertive voice. A voice without authority or adequate emphasis is asking to be interrupted.

A soft, quiet voice that lacks power is not only an invitation to be interrupted, it also implies, "I'm not very confident about what I'm saying, so I'm not going to say it very loudly." Sometimes it implies, "Maybe nobody will really hear this if I say it softly enough." That is the worst case scenario. But everyone knows what it sounds like to say something with great authority because it is backed by a strong belief. Women, when angry, can use that authority with a spouse or children. Not often enough, I think, can women use that same authoritative voice to say something powerfully to their colleagues, bosses, or even subordinates. A voice with authority is a voice that people listen to. (See Chapter Eight for more on effective vocal qualities.)

Have Inadequate Eye Contact

Inadequate or indirect eye contact hinders getting attention. For Americans generally, eye contact is closely associated with confidence, trust, and belief. The old expression, "He couldn't look me in the eye, so I don't think he's telling the truth," reflects this norm. Inability to look directly at the person to whom you are speaking diminishes your ability to get his attention when you speak. If you are looking down at your shoes or at the knot in his necktie rather than in his eyes, you will not get the quality of attention that you need. You set up in the listener's mind an image of someone who is not certain about what she is saying, who lacks confidence in its truth or validity or her strength of belief. (See Chapter Seven for tips on acting equal.)

Speech Mannerisms

Studies show, and my audiences of both men and women generally agree, that women

- ask more questions
- make statements in a questioning tone
- use more question tags
- lead off with a question
- use more hedges or qualifiers.

(These characteristics were first identified by Robin Lakoff, professor of linguistics at the University of California, in her milestone book, *Language and Women's Place*.)

Ask More Questions

A researcher analyzing tape-recorded conversations between professional couples found that women ask nearly three times as many questions as men (Fishman).

Clearly, asking questions indicates women's interest in listening. And women are the acknowledged champs as listeners. Because women ask so many questions and they are listening instead of talking, their point of view is not presented. As women are successful in encouraging others to state their opinions, they have less time and opportunity to make their own opinions known. When the communicators are male and female, and if the female asks three times as many questions, the man will make more statements, the woman fewer. If a woman wants her ideas taken seriously, one item of business is to be sure her ideas get presented.

Make Statements in a Questioning Tone

Questions naturally solicit the attention of a listener. Yet, when used frequently, this characteristic suggests lack of confidence in an idea. It suggests that you already anticipate the listener will not be listening. Intonation patterns in English demonstrate intent. Rising inflection is appropriate after a group of words that is a question; falling inflection signals a statement. If a rising inflection is put on a statement, it thus becomes a question. Consider this example: "I was walking by that new building?" Although the words are arranged like a statement, the intonation makes it a question. When it is recreated on paper such as this, it has a question mark at the end. As a variation on this theme, someone told of a Harvard study that indicates women tend to make statements followed by a laugh at the end. Though I could not locate the study, we all know many women who do this. This habit, too, reflects lack of confidence.

Use More Question Tags

This mannerism also signals lack of confidence. It suggests you have doubt about your statement. Samples of question tags include "...don't you?" "...haven't we?" "...should we?" tacked on to the end of a statement. "I believe the report should be approved, don't you?" "I don't think we should give Jamie her new bicycle yet, do you?" Many women make strong statements, only to weaken them with a question tag: "That is a good solution to the problem, don't you agree?" "The project should not be allowed to continue, should it?" "We should take mother out to dinner tonight, shouldn't we?" These tags turn a potentially effective statement into just another question.

Viewed as consensus building, as discussed above, this device does draw people out, because it encourages others to respond. It encourages dialogue to continue, while a statement often concludes a discussion. But if the goal is getting people to listen, it often signals lack of confidence in one's opinion. The question tag also signals an inability to express an opinion firmly. What is an asset in terms of consensus-building becomes a liability when getting people to take you seriously.

Lead Off With a Question

Women sometimes start a conversation with a phrase such as, "Hey, you know what?" Or, "Guess what happened today?" Or, "You'll never guess what happened today?"—again with rising inflection. While innocuous questions in themselves, when used as devices intended to insure a listener's attention they become problems because they, too, signal uncertainty and a desire for attention. The point will not be lost on readers that this is the way children begin conversations with adults, often accompanied by a tap on the knee or a tug at the sleeve. There is some comfort in the fact that most women refrain from tugging at the sleeve of their spouse or boss as they attempt to get attention, but using the question device as an attention-getting opener does leave a similar impression.

Use More Hedges or Qualifiers

Both research and testimonials indicate that women use more hedges and qualifiers in their speech than men do. Examples: "I *kind of* think this is a good idea." "We *probably* should do this, *don't you think?*" "It *seems* like a *fairly* good idea." One implication of qualifiers and hedging words is that you lack confidence in your idea or opinion. The other implication is a lack of courage to strongly state your belief. Imagine the different impact the Book of Genesis might have if it read, "And God saw that it was *kind of* good," (Genesis 1:25). What impact would the powerful Nike advertising slogan possess if it had said, "You probably should do it," instead of "Just Do It."

Communicating Tendencies

Other tendencies in women's communications, like the speech mannerisms, are strengths in some situations, harmful in others. First, consider this list of negative tendencies as they reflect failure to get the attention of listeners:

- use too many details
- fail to distinguish between important and trivial
- do not state opinions
- are not decisive.

Use Too Many Details

Women tend to like details. Women tend to see more details. Evidence shows that women are more observant, out of both necessity (as mothers) and interest. Tannen indicates that women tell details because details aid in establishing intimacy, a primary goal for women in conversation (p. 115). It is this abundant use of details—more than any other female communications trait—that men readily admit they find so irritating. And it is no wonder: given the widely analyzed and described understanding of men's fear of intimacy, it follows that they do not want women to share details, let alone avoid offering details themselves. (But that is another book.)

The inclusion of details as a way of building relationships can be a positive trait, even in business; it is a trait, and a skill, that men in business could adapt to better use. However, women tend to add details to a conversation even when the primary goal is not rapport building. What women can do is use better judgement about when to furnish those details. A committee report, for instance, is usually not an instance where rapport needs to be built.

Because they want more details, women tend to give them when asked about something. Women get frustrated when they ask about something and get a terse or short response. When prompted about a meeting or party, women tend to give what they would want, which is a full description. If you have one scintilla of doubt, listen to the amount of detail in conversations in the next few days (or hours) between two women. Hasn't every one of you holding this book right now had someone say to you recently, "Would you get to the point?" Or, "What is the point of this?" Or, "What are you trying to say?" Or, "What is it that you want?" My doctor's office manager exclaimed recently, "If only I had a nickel for every time my husband has said to me, 'Would you please get to the point!' And he wasn't asking it as a question, either."

According to Deborah Tannen, for women, talk is interaction; for men, talk is information (p. 81). It is no wonder, then, that men tend to prefer to hear just the nitty gritty, the bottom line, the result. And that is what they tend to give. Remember the story told about President Calvin Coolidge, known for being a man of especially few words. One Sunday when his wife was reportedly too ill to go to church, the President went alone. Upon his return she asked him what the sermon was about. He replied, "Sin." "Well," his wife persisted, "what did he say about sin?" "He was against it," Coolidge responded.

As an interesting sidelight to the importance of details to women, it has been my experience that women—even in a business setting—are often able to keep a conversation going on several levels at the same time. This skill both irritates men and frustrates them, possibly because they are less able to accomplish it. Consider this dialogue between two executive-level women at a business lunch:

Linda: *…so what we need in this training is to develop a sense of usefulness and rapport. The support staff is feeling left out of the loop these days.*

Mandy: *Yeah, there's a lot of that going around. I've heard something similar from a couple of clients in Seattle recently. When I was in Seattle I had lunch with Yvonne. She looks great … tanned, rested. She's sure happy to be out of the corporate world for awhile. She said, "Hi."*

Linda: *What's she doing? Just taking some time off?*

Mandy: *No, she was working on a book, sitting up on top of her houseboat. Yeah, I guess she is kinda taking some time off!*

Linda: *What approach would you suggest for getting our telephones answered with more professionalism and instilling a sense of being needed? Sounds like two different sessions.*

Mandy: *That's easy, I think. We'll use a group problem-solving approach. People in small groups will interact well and everybody gets a chance to participate. Each group can have a specific problem on telephone usage to solve. You've got some of those, haven't you?*

Linda: *Do we ever. Talk about problems on the phone. I can't get my teenager to give up the line for three minutes these days. I think she has a new boyfriend, but she's not talking. At least to me! What about the "feeling needed" part?*

Mandy: *You'll be the last to know about the new boyfriend, won't you. Isn't that a kick! I can start off with a high-minded pitch—you know what I mean—to make them feel needed, and then draw them into the problem solving. And they know their image on the phone is important.*

Linda: *Sounds good. I'll get a letter out to confirm it in a day or two. Two hours ought to be enough? These days teenagers can't even decide what to wear in two hours! I remember calling my girlfriend to be sure we were all going to wear white pants to school on Friday, but they seem to have more decisions to make these days.*

Mandy: *I'm sure our folks thought exactly the same about us. It'll be interesting to work with your staff ... 60, did you say?*

These two women have successfully dealt with the issue of lunch—upcoming training. They also shared news of a mutual friend and of their families, and enjoyed a laugh about their own teenage years, all reinforcing their own relationship.

It has been said that men see the forest and describe it. Women see the trees and describe not only the trees, but every leaf on every branch and the dirt underneath the trees. It is easy to see why both genders are frustrated!

In two important areas, being listened to and creating successful conversations, the approach that men tend to prefer succeeds more often than women's. As I have described in Chapter Two of *Thinking on Your Feet*, there is a contract that people fulfill in a successful conversation.

> *Successful communications—any conversa-
> tion, social or business—involves an unspoken
> contract between the participating parties. This
> contract has two conditions: 1) both people
> want the communication to succeed, and 2)
> both people contribute to the communication.
> The result is a layering effect, a building of the
> information pool. Each listens and then adds to
> what the other has said.*

If, when asked about a meeting or party, you give
too many details all at once, you violate the contract
by denying the other a chance to contribute. With
patience, it is possible to gradually share most details
you would like to by building a conversation.

Fail to Distinguish Between
the Important and Trivial

The second problem is that women tend,
through their detailed description of a situation, to
fail to distinguish between the important and the un-
important. Some of this failure to distinguish what is
important comes from wanting to share what you
saw, observed, and felt in great detail. It may also
come from an inability to recognize the significant
findings or results. It also reflects an unwillingness to
prioritize the information. The simple solution is the
old formula of "Need to Know; Nice to Know; Don't
Need to Know." See Chapter Five for a more detailed
plan for making decisions about relative importance.

Imagine this scenario: Your colleague has been
unable to attend a meeting. He comes to your desk

after the meeting and asks, "How did the meeting go?" That is an open-ended question, and as such it implies he wants a full, general explanation of the meeting. Do not be misled. He does not want a full, general explanation; what he wants is: "It was a successful meeting. We decided to postpone the sales presentation for a week. John will get back to us about the details."

What women tend to say instead is

> *Well, it was really an interesting meeting. Needless to say, everybody had a lot to talk about, and Ralph, as usual, gave his regular speech on how we never get anything done on time. Martha sat there sulking in the corner like she always does because she couldn't get her words in edgewise. It seemed clear that we're obviously not ready to make the thing happen, and so after a lot of discussion about why, the supervisor said it looks like we ought to table this thing for a while. I wonder what you think we ought to do about getting it rescheduled, but nearly everybody realized we needed to have a time-line, so what we decided to do was meet in a week to see if we were ready.*

To summarize these gender-related characteristics, it has been said that women tend to speak in paragraphs, while men tend to speak in sentences. While a simplistic statement, it does capture the inability of women to separate important from trivial, which results in too many details.

Don't State Opinions

Women tend to exhibit an inability or perhaps an unwillingness to express a clear opinion, even if that opinion is specifically requested. This is reflected in question tags (see Speech Mannerisms above). It is also reflected in lack of emphasis in voice (see above, Non-Verbal Traits). Finally, it is demonstrated through hedging (see Speech Mannerisms above).

Part of the quality that makes women good consensus builders also contributes to a lack of ability to express firm opinions. Some people feel that a firm opinion tends to close a discussion. But it shouldn't. If asked "Do you think we should continue a radio campaign for this product?" a woman is apt to say, *Well, the radio advertising has got some good results. We know that there are 20 percent more calls and inquiries, but you know, it's been going on for quite a long time and maybe it's getting stale. What do you think?*

If the seeker had wanted you to summarize the pros and cons, she would have asked you for a summary. She asked for your opinion.

Look at the question again: "Do you think we should continue a radio campaign for this product?" The answer should be, "Yes, I believe we should," or "No, I think a change is in order." Remember, the option for follow-up questions is both easy and appropriate. They are easy because people simply have to ask for more details if they want them. They are appropriate because you build a conversation that way.

If your spouse calls to ask if you want to go out to dinner, believe that he does indeed care what your wishes are. Say, "Yes, let's." Or, "I'm too tired to go out. Would you be a love and pick up Chinese?"

What is happening in these situations is sometimes a failure to listen carefully to the question. If women are good listeners, they must listen accurately and draw conclusions, not just mirror thoughts and build consensus at all times.

Are Not Decisive

Women tend to waffle when asked to make decisions. I was chatting last summer with the chairperson of a huge Northwest writers' conference. She needed additional volunteers for a project. Her list contained the names of six men and six women. As she made her calls, she got a definite yes or no from each of the six men and an indefinite "maybe" from each of the six women. The women said, "H-mm, that would be interesting, but I'm really busy." Or "I'd like to. Give me a day or two to think about it and I'll call you back." Or, "How soon do you have to know?" While not a definitive study, this reflects a recognizable tendency in women's communications. My experience as volunteer coordinator of a nonprofit organization replicates her experience. I cannot remember a time I have received an unqualified yes or no from a woman whom I have approached for a task. The men have responded somewhat more definitely.

While women's communications style has much that is effective, some of those effective aspects hinder their ability to be effective in getting listened to. The two key elements for gaining that initial attention are getting to the point quickly and prioritizing information. The goal is *not* to talk like men, but to talk in ways that facilitate dialogue—and, in times when power is needed, be able to talk equal to powerful men.

CHAPTER FOUR

It's an Age Issue

In a hurry?

- *pick your spots*
- *stick to one issue*
- *give one example*

Getting others to listen is also an age issue. Older people tell me they are especially frustrated when trying to communicate with younger people, especially their adult children. Older people feel they have lots to offer, having experienced so much of life. Their plaint is, "Why won't anybody listen to me?" Younger people tend to respond—to paraphrase an old television commercial—"Please, mother, I'd rather learn it myself!"

It is entirely logical that the older you get the more knowledge you probably have and the more experiences you can bring to bear on a given situation.

It is equally apparent to practically everyone that younger people are not interested in the experiences, and only slightly more willing to accept the knowledge. We all want to cut our own path.

Yet parents have spent a great portion of their lives nurturing, guiding, and protecting their children; as people get older, the desire and the need to nurture, guide, and protect apparently does not diminish much. What to do? The best advice is the same advice: you cannot change other people; you can change only yourself. Older people can, by altering certain habits, increase the chance that their advice or counsel will be heeded.

Pick Your Spots

Most of the time when you would like to offer advice, don't. My older friends and relatives tell me that hardly a moment goes by when they wouldn't like to offer a suggestion. The logic is simple—the fewer times you offer advice, the more likely you are to be listened to when you do offer it. Save what clout you have for the important issues. It does not matter if the potatoes get brown because your daughter-in-law peels them too early and does not remember to cover them with water. Nothing of importance will befall the world because your son leaves the newspapers lying around after he reads them. Let his wife nag him about that. Do not tell your grandson that his mother will shout at him if he leaves his ball and mitt on the stairs again. You are not his mother; let her parent him.

You have been able to bite your tongue during these trivial incidents. So when you do speak up about wasting water, you just may get their attention. Avoid a monologue about how they are wasting water by running it full blast when brushing their teeth or rinsing the dishes. Mention conserving resources; try to get a dialogue going.

The choosing of issues is equally important when you are speaking up in a business, association or organizational setting, either professional or civic. If you have been involved in business for many years, you have met and come to grips with a great many issues that younger associates still have to learn about. Let them learn. Save your counsel for key issues. I know an extremely savvy man who now finds himself the oldest member of his professional organization. He recognizes that the younger members do not really want to hear him tell about the old days, "how we used to do it." He keeps his own counsel during business and strategy meetings, picking his spots and speaking up for key issues. He is listened to when he does speak. The less you offer, the more likely it is to be heard.

Consider these additional tips, which will sound familiar, because they are essentially the same tips for getting anyone to listen at any time:

- get to the point early
- stick to one issue
- use one example
- stop.

Get to the Point Early

You will recognize this as the same advice found throughout. Use the direct approach. Put your point up front rather than burying it at the end of lengthy explanation. You improve your chances of that point being heard. The lengthy explanation leads to, "Get to the point" or "What is it you are trying to say?" Empirical evidence suggests that, probably out of respect, adult children are less likely to state it, but they do think it. The familiar glazed-over eyes are common.

Stick to One Issue

This advice, important for anyone who wants to be listened to, is crucial for older talkers; when many issues are brought up in one conversation, it is easy for the younger person to simply write off his or her parent as confused. Here is a sample of a damaging, multi-issue comment:

> I don't know why you can't get all the groceries I asked you for at one time. I asked you to make a list, but, oh, no, you have such a good memory you don't need a list. You were just as stubborn as a child. You never would remember to bring the note home from the teacher even though I asked you to put it in the front pocket of your shirt where I would at least find it when

I did the laundry. You'll have to go back to the store.

Here's a better way to get attention for what you want: "Here's my grocery list. Writing the list helps me keep track of things I need, and you'll be able to get everything in just one trip."

One elderly friend of mine is working, with my suggestions, at getting better responses from her doctors and other health care workers. Here's the way she used to begin:

You wanted me to let you know how if the new pills were making me nervous. Well, I'm a nervous wreck. I get so jittery that I want to scream. None of the girls who come to help me understand that I'm so nervous. They keep telling me to just relax. Young girls today know nothing about sick people. When I was a girl, we were taught to be respectful to elderly people and sick people, too. That's another problem, I can't get your receptionist to understand that I just can't wait around for appointments. She doesn't seem to realize how sick I am.

Now when she wants to make a complaint or ask a question, she organizes beforehand, trying to focus on one problem or issue at a time. If there are several, she verbally counts them, like this, "I have three problems that I want to ask you about today. First ...." She accomplishes several goals with this counting structure: first, she lets the doctor know how many issues are coming up; second, she keeps herself focused better with good support for her points; third, she demonstrates clarity of mind by not wandering or mixing issues.

She plans what she is going to say, and it comes out something like this:

> *Dr. Beamer, there are two things I need to talk with you about. First, I'm very nervous, and second, I am having trouble getting my care workers to do what I ask them to do. About the nerves. About half an hour after I take the new pills, I feel a tingling sensation and...*

The difference is striking. Yet it is not that difficult to do. Try counting and sorting issues with your own doctor, or your children.

Use One Example

When you want to support a point, do so. But select the best example and limit yourself to it. Planning to use only one example helps you to remain focused on what the important issue is. That will also help your listener to remain focused, too. Also, you will be less likely to digress.

Stop

(Is that clear?)

Special Problems

Certain types of examples and explanations are special turn-offs. First among these are historical stories, because the desire to relate details causes the stories to be too long virtually every time. It is possible to cite your experience so that your listener understands that you are talking from an actual event. Do so in a single sentence, such as this: "That happened to me when I was working with the Post Office," or "I had that same trouble during the trip we took to Alaska one summer." This approach lets the other person know that you have an experience to share. You are encouraging a dialogue. The other person may ask a follow-up question if he or she is interested. If no follow-up questions are asked, no dialogue is begun, you have been spared the discomfort of telling a long story that nobody paid attention to.

Another serious turn-off for younger people is "used to" phrases: "When I was your age we used to..." or "I used to..." The reaction of your younger listener, whether stated or merely thought, is likely to be, "But times have changed" or "We have better equipment now" or "But I don't care what you used to do. I'm doing it my way." Harsh? Yes. But, candidly, how many people at any age enjoy receiving advice? Don't all raise your hands at once!

A third potential problem for older talkers is a way of speaking or a tone of voice that has a whining quality. This aspect of vocal quality is probably not something your adult child will mention to you. Monitor yourself. Listen to your older friends who have a whine in their voice to remind yourself that you do not want to sound that way. See Chapter Eight for more on vocal qualities.

CHAPTER FIVE

It's a Power Issue

In a hurry?

• *say less than you want to say*
• *say it assertively*

Power is described by the *American Heritage Dictionary of the English Language* as, "the ability or capacity to act or perform effectively." That definition directs this discussion of speech and communication characteristics into the ability to be powerful. People who get the attention of others are able to act effectively. People who are heard have power. People who have an opinion and can express it so it is received and given recognition are powerful people—male or female. Power should not be either a gender issue or an age issue. Still, to the extent that society sees it as a gender issue, women need to view it that way too. Women can gain power by enhancing their abilities to talk effectively. Men who feel they do not command attention when they talk can enhance their power by following the same guidelines. To the extent that older people feel powerless, they can gain power by speaking more effectively (see Chapter Four).

Powerful people know what they want to say. They say it in a concise, precise manner. They say it with force and with emphasis in their voice. They say it with good eye contact. They say it with good posture. They say it with assertive body language and assertive behavior. They avoid subordinate non-verbal behavior and speech mannerisms that weaken their effectiveness.

It is possible to be listened to, to get your message across, without developing and using every one of these traits or characteristics. But when any one of them is missing, an extra barrier or obstacle is put between the speaker and the listener. It is the speaker's responsibility to overcome the obstacle. It is much easier to prevent the barriers by adopting the speaking habits and patterns of powerful people.

Consider these habits of powerful people:

- recognize how power acts
- speak to the perspective of the audience
- get to the point
- avoid ineffective communication characteristics
- practice strong non-verbal behavior
- recognize that equality is a part of power.

Recognize How Power Acts

Studies abound which analyze power. One New York women's sports foundation analyzed types of power in ways that facilitate our understanding of how communications traits project power. They classified types of power in two ways: hierarchy power and individual power. Hierarchy power includes 1) position in the organization, 2) authority and responsibility, and 3) resources under your control. Individual power includes 1) interpersonal competence, 2) task competence, and 3) charisma.

Their study showed that men tend to use all three aspects of hierarchy power plus charisma. Women tend to use only interpersonal and task competence. Their findings suggest that men

- *tell* subordinates what to do and how to do it
- push their ideas through
- assume deference to authority.

Women, on the other hand, tend to

- set general guidelines and empower subordinates
- build consensus for their ideas
- presume that deference to authority should be earned.

Dr. Tannen indicates that men function in a world where power and accomplishments form the hierarchy; women function in a world whose hierarchy is formed primarily through friendship and community (p. 25). The male power style is visible and assertive. It tends to produce fast action, but does not encourage colleagueship, shared responsibility, or co-operation. One of my clients, a powerful male whose profession is management consulting, had this to say upon hearing about the topic of this book: "Males are more action-oriented and less deliberative." Another powerful male client said, "Men tend to be more directive and less concerned about consensus building." Because female power is less visible, it takes more time to emerge. It encourages cooperation and fosters long-term results. The fact that female power focuses on consensus building is reinforced by women's communications characteristics as described in Chapter Three.

This research relates to your purpose—getting people to listen to you—in two ways: first, it reinforces that the communication characteristics of both men and women are reflected in how they assume power. Second, it relates to the ideas below on the importance of speaking to the perspective of the audience you hope to reach. To do this, you first make an assessment of that audience. Recognizing the approaches to power that men and women use will enable you to make a gender-specific assessment of that audience.

A gender-specific assessment would include the ways that each gender uses power. If your audience is male or largely male, you can be more direct and more specific in recognition of men's tendency to tell people what to do, to push their ideas through, and to assume that their authority is being deferred to. If your audience is largely or wholly women, your best approach will interact with the audience more quickly and more frequently, getting involvement and building consensus for your ideas. Further assessment follows the usual lines: consider education, position, profession, political leanings, knowledge of your topic, and interest in the topic.

Use The Communications Triangle (below) to quickly assess the relationships between you as teller, the message to be told, and the audience.

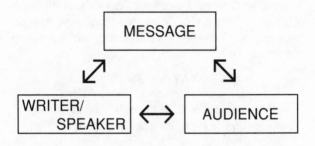

The Communications Triangle
© 1979, Marian K. Woodall

Speak to the Perspective of the Audience

To be successful in getting the attention of an audience—one person or a group—coming from their perspective will usually contribute to your success, and thus to your power. Coming from their perspective means focusing first on their needs. It means couching your ideas in language they understand, using examples and details they relate to. That strategy will ensure you get their attention: when you are talking about them, they will listen, and listen intently. When you begin talking about yourself first, you fail to gain their interest.

In my book *Speaking to a Group*, the importance of presenting from the perspective of the audience is discussed extensively. Failure to consider your audience first is highlighted as the greatest error made in public speaking:

> *Audience appropriateness is everything. It's not what could be said to this audience, it's what should be said to them. It's not what you want them to know, it's what they are willing to hear, what they want to hear, or what they will sit still for.* (Woodall, p. 36.)

Failure to understand this essential truth, that everything comes from the perspective of the audience, creates problems in public speaking, whether it be sales presentations, staff morale speeches, fund raisers, or awards ceremonies.

Transfer this advice to giving individuals particular information. Talk about yourself first, you will not gain their attention. Talk about them first, get them involved; then you can move smoothly to your agenda, building discussion with an involved participant.

Imagine that person sitting across from you as you begin to talk, thinking, "So?" Or musing, "Well, what's in it for me?" Make sure there is something in it for him. Consider this personal example:

Our yard is home to an extensive rose garden. My spouse and I share the numerous tasks necessary to keep it in good condition. One of his tasks is taking care of their long-term health. His goal is to prevent diseases and insects. He also treats the problems he hasn't prevented. At the heart of his program is a systemic, which feeds the plants as well as providing fungicide and insecticide. If this application is made in a timely manner (every six weeks), the rest of the health care is easier. But he has trouble being timely.

Here are two ways I have approached it. The typical nagging-wife approach goes something like this:

> *It's past time to do the roses again. I wrote it on the calendar, hoping that you'd do it without my having to remind you. I reminded you twice last week. I wish just once you'd do it without my having to push on it, dear.*

Does that sound familiar? (And is it any wonder he doesn't listen and the roses stay sick?)

Here is the "how to talk so men will listen" version:

> *You know how much you hate spraying the roses. Using the systemic regularly will save you a lot of spraying. It's been six weeks, so it's time.*

The second approach puts the emphasis on "What's in it for me?" I get the attention I need, and so do the roses.

That same sense of audience reflects a basic strategy that is easy to understand, because it relates to buying and selling: You don't sell the features of your piece of equipment or service, you sell the benefits to the particular person. Selling features speaks from your perspective. Employing this strategy means thinking about what that persons wants, needs, or can deal with, and then speaking to that perspective. It is easy to recognize the audience perspective in sales: A bank would be selling features if it advertised, "We have 24 Automatic Teller Machines in the metropolitan area." More wisely, it sells benefits by touting, "You can get cash whenever you need it at an ATM near your home or office."

In other words, say first what the audience wants to hear, not what you want to say. When you say what you want to say, you may be getting something off your chest or championing your cause. But if the audience does not listen to it, you will not have succeeded in communicating. It is helpful to remember that communication is a process that involves the listener not only hearing the information but also receiving it.

Does this mean you should never express your strong opinions from your personal viewpoint? No, it does not mean that. It does mean that if you wish to be listened to, consider what perspective that audience has. Get their involvement first and work your strong opinions in second.

Get to the Point

Taking too long to get to the point is a key error that people seeking to be more powerful need to avoid. The most significant error is that you waste people's time. Failure to sift the details to find the key points is the biggest problem. Too often the listener is drowned with information. The solution is easy: Present the highlights and stop. People can ask follow-up questions if they want more details. You probably will not be surprised that few people want more than the highlights.

Consider a report or explanation of an activity, an event, or a request you want to make. There are two primary types of reports you could give. One is an historical report (what I call an "and then we..." report) the other is a results-focused or "bottom line" report.

In any event or situation there are several key questions: *What happened? When did it happen? Who was involved? Why did it happen? What were the results? What will the repercussions be?* The powerful person automatically divides the information into three categories: Need To Know, Nice To Know, and Don't Need to Know.

In an historical report (the kind that ineffective people tend to give), all these aspects are mentioned and many are thoroughly described. In an historic report the explainer seldom attempts to differentiate between the important and the trivial: it all comes out equally. Here is a sample:

We just got a call from ABC Corporation. They were very upset because they didn't get a complete shipment and they had a sales circular out and everyone was extremely unhappy. I tried to figure out what was the matter and finally traced it down to the fact that somebody simply transposed a couple of numbers. It seemed important to solve the customer's problem, so I took it upon myself to call them and tell them that I was shipping the extra cartons air freight rather than our usual overland route, and then after some consultation, I suggested to our staff that all future orders be written by one person and cross-checked by another person, instead of the way we do now, as you know, which is to have one person write and initial the cross-check at the same time.

In an historical report (the kind that ineffective people tend to give), all three categories of information are included, and often thoroughly described. Need-to-Know information is side by side with Don't-Need-to-Know information.

In a results-oriented report, on the other hand, most if not all attention is given to the final two questions, *Why did it happen? What are the repercussions?* These are the bottom line. The speaker takes it upon herself to decide the "Need-to-Know" information. The "Nice-to-Know" details will be available if they are requested. The "Don't-Need-to-Know" tidbits are just that. Here is the same report, results-oriented:

The incomplete shipment of ABC Corporation was the result of a transposition of two numbers. We took two steps: called the client to say that the missing cartons were arriving by air freight at no extra charge; and requested that future orders be written by one person and cross-checked by another.

To get the attention of your listener, decide how much information to present. Whether you have a report or a request, the same assessment, the same decisions, need to be made—if you want to be listened to. That is fine for business, you are thinking. But what about at home? When my spouse asks how my day went, do I have to sift the details and group every little item by Need to Know and Nice to Know? Perhaps. If you are reading this book, my assumption is that your spouse is not avidly hooked on your every word! Try this: Select the most significant, funny, unusual, trying, or demanding aspect of your day's activities. Lead off with that—briefly. Your spouse will probably pick up on it, asking a question or adding a comment. What have you done? You have begun building a dialogue. After he is involved, you can tell other interesting items.

Avoid Ineffective Communication Characteristics

Subordinate speech mannerisms for unpowerful people include a litany similar to that which women fall prey to when they are not confident in their message and not assertive in their delivery (see Chapter Three):

- questioning too much; stating too little
- making statements with a questioning tone
- using question tags to demonstrate lack of certainty
- using a question-like statement to gain the attention of an inattentive listener
- hedging instead of making firm statements.

All these mannerisms demonstrate a lack of confidence. To be powerful, people must be confident. Having clear opinions is the first step. Expressing them forthrightly and assertively is the second step. You must appear and sound confident to inspire confidence in others. To paraphrase an old saying, "No one is ever going to be more confident about you than you are about yourself." See Chapter Six for more on confidence.

Practice Strong Non-Verbal Behavior

Unpowerful non-verbal behavior includes virtually the same problems that were described in Chapter Three. To counteract these self-defeating non-verbal messages, develop these strong habits:

- discourage interruptions
- use a resonant, confident voice
- establish and maintain strong eye contact.

Recognize That Equality is a Part of Power

If being powerful means acting effectively, one key for greater success is to recognize you are equal to the people or person to whom you are speaking. The mind-set that says, "I don't think I'm very important...I don't think my opinion matters very much...I'm a woman...I'm only a secretary...I'm just support staff...I'm the most junior person on the team" does not enable a person to effectively demonstrate necessary powerful verbal and non-verbal qualities. This mind set also does not enable a person to avoid the subordinate speech mannerisms and communications characteristics that accompany in-effectiveness.

How can you become powerful by demonstrating equality?

- feel like an equal
- act like an equal
- sound like an equal
- look like an equal.

CHAPTER SIX

Feel Like an Equal

In a hurry?

- *equality starts in your head*

How can you demonstrate equality? Equality is a state of mind and a state of body. Equality is reflected in your verbal and non-verbal communications. The first step in being more powerful—in being listened to—is to feel like an equal. Consider these three goals:

- be confident in yourself
- be confident in your message
- know what you want.

Achieving these goals will set you on the road to equality and to power. These goals will help you achieve your larger goal—being listened to.

Be Confident in Yourself

Equality must start in your mind. Remind yourself you have a right to be where you are. In most instances, you became a part of that situation in the same way all the others did. You were hired, appointed, selected, or chosen for the position. Or you selected or chose your spot. You are in an equal relationship or marriage. So you begin equal. Letting that equality slip away, or worse yet, not ever capitalizing on it, can be your undoing.

A most revealing example of the importance of reminding yourself that you have a right to be where you are occurred after a recent speech. A woman of about thirty came up to me. She was dressed in jeans, a nice blouse, and sneakers. She said, "Marian, I have an especially difficult problem. I wonder if you could give me a few minutes." It turned out that she was the designated student representative on a search committee for a new college president. All the other members of the search committee were faculty members, business people, or civic leaders. She had two concerns: would she be accepted, and how should she address these people, particularly the chairman of the board, Mr. David Jones.

I paused, looked her over, and responded, "First, you need to believe that you have a right to be there, and second, you need to dress like it." She grimaced slightly and said, "I don't have expensive suits." My advice: "Wear the most professional outfit you own. The best way to be accepted by the members of this committee is to look as much like them as possible.

Assume that you have a right to be there. Walk in strongly. Shake hands with each one, every time. Address each person by his or her last name the first time, because that's appropriate in any situation. Most of those people will say, as the chairman is apt to say, 'Please call me David.'" She smiled, in recognition that feeling equal will help her act and sound equal.

Be confident you are an equal whenever you participate in a meeting, a conference, or a conversation in your family. Be confident in the specific situation where you are about to make a statement or a request, *expecting* that a specific someone will listen.

Confidence counts in every way. As indicated in earlier chapters, it affects the way you speak, the way you put together sentences, the way you use your vocal instrument, and the effect you have on others whom you want to listen to you. You must be confident.

Be Confident in Your Message

You must also have confidence in your specific message. To have that, prepare the message ahead of time. Do not try to wing it. Think about what you are going to say; reassure yourself it is worth saying. Be sure it will add significantly or importantly or at least adequately to what is being discussed. Get directly to your point. Learn not to bring up old experiences and war stories. If the point of general discussion is passed, do not go backward to state something no longer helpful. If specifics are being asked for, don't offer a generalization. If opinions are being sought, offer one.

Whenever you begin to speak, either in business or social situations, if you just open your mouth and allow whatever occurs to you to come out, you are not doing the preparation necessary to be confident that your words will make a contribution. Know what you want to say.

Know What You Want

You also need to know what you want. Why are you about to make that statement or ask that question? For confirmation? For approval? Seeking consensus? Wanting to be acknowledged as a significant player? Hoping for a vote? Simply indicating that you are listening and on top of the situation? Trying to show you are part of a team? Indicating your opinion has changed? Demonstrating you are willing to proceed? Expressing a new direction? Offering an alternative to what has already been said? Know *what* you want to say and *why* you want to say it. (There is more about *how* to say it in Chapter Eight.)

Your feeling of equality will be enhanced by these assessments of your message. It is not easy to make an assessment quickly, but you can learn to do it and do it well. Having done so will enhance your confidence. Your confidence will further enhance your feeling of equality. It will also strengthen your ability to act like an equal, as discussed in the next chapter.

CHAPTER SEVEN

Act Like an Equal

In a hurry?

- *stand up to speak*
- *make eye contact*

Use non-verbal communications to project the confidence you feel. Act equal. Once you recognize what you have to say is important, you can move beyond the subordinate behavior and approval-seeking actions that doom your statements to the failure of not being listened to. Consider these actions to enhance your power and your ability to get listened to:

- stand up
- avoid subordinate speech mannerisms
- use strong gestures
- have assertive posture
- establish eye contact
- use touch effectively.

Stand Up

If the situation is important to you, stand up to speak. Several changes occur when you stand up. First, your voice will be louder and firmer. You will use the entire delivery instrument—your body. You will use more effective gestures naturally. You will create a more emphatic effect. You will eliminate the possibility that you are slumping in a subordinate manner or sitting back in your chair, wishing yourself into the background like a piece of the wallpaper. You will get people's attention, partly because other people have not stood as they made their comments.

On hearing my strongly worded comment that she should stand when making a presentation to her board of directors, a client recently blurted out, "But everyone will look at me!" I smiled and replied, "Naturally, that's the idea."

Noted professional speech trainer, Paul LeRoux, author of *Selling To A Group*, summarizes it nicely:

> *When we really want to make a point, we do it best standing. We're more dominating, especially if others are seated. We appear more forceful because we use larger gestures and speak more loudly. When you stand, you and your message are the center of attention.* (LeRoux, p. 3)

If you doubt the wisdom—and the power—of standing, try it out. In your next few meetings, conferences with your boss, and conversations with your spouse, try both—speak your piece once seated and the next time standing. You will feel more in control, more powerful, more equal, when standing. You may also feel uncomfortable. Any new activity, any change, is bound to cause some discomfort. That is all right. We're talking about *change* here.

My clients say there is an instant feeling of greater strength and power when they are standing. A powerful female attorney heard this presentation; she was struck by my emphasis on the importance of standing when introducing yourself at a lunch or meeting. After trying it only once she felt stronger, but a tad self-conscious; after the second successful standing introduction she felt more comfortable and lost the self-conscious feeling. Now she stands. Now she feels powerful out of the courtroom as well as in.

Some people "sort of" stand when introducing themselves at group luncheons and network sessions. You know the motion: they begin talking before they are fully standing, they rapidly spit out their name and company, then begin to resume their seat half-way through the description of their business. You also know how they sound: "HimynameisMarian-Woodall-with-Prfessnal-Busns-Cmmcations." They bob up and down as if they were on a spring. They usually look down at the table as they talk. Their voice is thus not directed out toward the audience, and they cannot be heard beyond the second table. They typically speak too rapidly. They do not act equal to anyone, especially to powerful people.

Test the confident feeling that comes from standing. When it is your turn, stand up and push back your chair, all the while keeping your mouth closed. Once you are fully erect, look out toward the most distant part of the audience, but continue to keep your mouth closed. After you have established eye contact with someone at the far table, with a firm voice say, "Would you like to be a more powerful speaker? [Pause.] I'm Marian Woodall, professional speech coach and president of Professional Business Communications. [Pause.] Call me to become more powerful." (More about the content of this kind of introduction in Chapter Eight.) Only after you have finished the last word do you then begin to lower your body back toward the chair. Try it, you'll like it!

An easy test is to pay attention to how people introduce themselves at meetings, conferences, or luncheons. You can note how much firmer voices are when people stand. You will easily see how standing up enhances the effects of equality and power.

Avoid Subordinate Speech Mannerisms

All the subordinate behavior described in Chapter Three needs to be monitored and overcome for you to act equal:

- avoid approval seeking
- avoid question tags
- avoid intensifiers and qualifiers
- avoid rising inflection.

You made the decision to speak and assessed your comment as important, useful, or helpful. You have the confidence you need. You do not need approval-seeking devices; you have already given yourself approval. You do not need reinforcement devices such as hedging or qualifiers when you have a strong message. The intensity in your voice and the emphasis on important words will provide the reinforcement.

Use Strong Gestures

Use strong, effective gestures. Gestures are natural. They mirror or reinforce the words and the emotion that you feel. You will use appropriate gestures naturally when you are standing and when you believe in what you say. Being able to move your hands and arms about in an expansive way demonstrates a sense of confidence and freedom. "Freedom" is obvious: when standing you will have hands and arms available above the table.

Think about gestures in two categories—emphatic gestures and descriptive gestures. Emphatic gestures are those that reinforce the significance of what you are saying. Examples include raising your fist in the air in a gesture of power or holding up three fingers to indicate three points you wish to make.

Descriptive gestures include those motions to accompany phrases that actually have you sketching or painting pictures in the air. If you say, for example, "Everyone in this room needs to be responsible for a cleaner environment," your arm will naturally sweep across the breadth of the audience. Or, "Sometimes when I stand up to speak, I feel ten feet high," you will measure your hand way above your head.

Many of my clients worry about their gestures. They want help to find appropriate gestures. And help is available, though they usually discover that the help was not necessary. Why? Gestures are a natural part of communicating. Try this experiment: put a mirror near where you talk on the telephone, either at work or at home. As you are involved in conversations on the telephone, glance up at the mirror. If you are like most people, you will observe natural, spontaneous gestures, reinforcing your words and your tone.

These same natural, spontaneous gestures, both the emphatic and the descriptive, will occur when you are standing to make a point or introduce yourself—provided that your hands are free so they can move easily. In some miraculous way the brain sends signals down through your arms and out to your hands that logically reinforce the words that the brain is simultaneously sending out your mouth.

If you are concerned about gestures, there are some ways to practice them. Certain kinds of words encourage gestures.

- Number words—*first, second, third.*
- Words that indicate size—*the whole group, everyone, all of you, only those people on the left.*
- Direction words—*top, bottom, left, right, all around me, behind me, clear up to the ceiling, way out to the left.*
- Adverbs—*slowly, rapidly, hurriedly, lazily.* Adverb words tell how something is done, and you can very frequently supplement the how with a gesture of the appropriate feeling or mood.

- Verbs are motion words—he *raced* across the room, he *crept* slowly up to my desk, he *cowered* in front of me.
- Descriptions of people and things—*it was just a mess ... he cowered in front of my desk like a little boy...she stood in front of my desk with all the confidence in the world.* You can visualize what cowering at the desk like a little boy might look like and you can make your body do that. You can visualize what standing with great confidence in front of someone looks like and you can make your body do that. (Woodall, *Speaking to a Group*, 146.)

Have Assertive Posture

Changing your posture can change the way you feel about yourself. Go into your bedroom or bathroom where there is a large mirror and practice some different kinds of postures. Pull a chair up in front of your mirror and sit in a passive way, with your feet tucked under the chair, your hands folded in your lap, and your body slumped forward. See what an unpowerful picture you are presenting.

Now, move back in your chair. Sit up straight. Throw your shoulders back. Cross your legs, put your arms on the chair arms, and look out confidently. Smile. Hold your head up. Make sure your chin is up. Mark the contrast that you are presenting in these two postures.

Next, try standing as passively as you can, with your hands together in front of you, your shoulders slumped, your head forward. See what a pathetic picture that is. Transfer the assertive posture to your standing position. Stand with your feet slightly apart, arms naturally at your sides, shoulders back, and lean slightly forward. You will feel grounded. You will feel in control of your body. You will look powerful.

Establish Eye Contact

Women tend to have more trouble making eye contact, especially with men, than do their male counterparts. Perhaps that is because women have been taught to be subordinate, taught to look down. It may be because someone told women that they looked "cute" when they acted coy.

In our culture direct eye contact is as important as a firm handshake. (In some cultures it is disrespectful for women to make eye contact with men or with any authority figures.) If you have trouble making eye contact, here is an interesting exercise that you can practice with a few friends—perhaps in a professional or civic group—that will help to improve your eye contact.

Ask a few friends (three is the minimum) to sit or stand with you in a small group. Arrange with each of them to give you a small hand signal when you have looked at them for three or four seconds. Then tell a story. Talk about something you have done or give your opinions about some issue. Begin by looking at the first person and continue talking directly to that person until she unobtrusively signals you with her hand that you have spent four seconds with her. Then move on to the next person. Look directly into that person's eyes and talk to him until he gives you the signal that you have spoken four seconds, and so on around the group.

After you have been from one to the next around the group a time or two, get more adventuresome and look first to one side of the group, then the other side, and finally, to the center. In other words, make eye contact randomly among the group of people. Do this as many different times as you need to, until you are comfortable looking at people directly. Recognize they do give you reinforcement, they mirror what you are saying, they give you encouragement, and they contribute to your confidence.

Use Touch Effectively

An article called "Reach Out And ...," by Jill Neimark in the February 1985 issue of *Savvy* magazine indicated, "Touch makes the point clearly, touch is a strong communications tool that often goes unused." Her major point is that touch is a privilege of power. According to psychologist Nancy Henley of the University of California at Los Angeles, "Touching expresses dominance.... One will touch if one has or is attempting control over another" (p. 42).

Because of problems of sexual harassment, people are appropriately more conscious of being careful about touch. And it is absolutely vital that you recognize, whether you are male or female, that touch can be misconstrued. However, touching is an important tool of non-verbal communicating, and, carefully used, it can be an appropriate part of the communicating package.

A slight, quick touch, a tap, actually, is very difficult to construe as sexual or even intimate. It is certainly possible to use touch as a means of getting attention with equals, and even with your superior, if you have a sense that your relationship allows touch as a part of communicating behavior.

As a rule, touch travels down. That is, people are more apt to touch subordinates than they are to touch superiors. Jessie Potter, Director of the National Institute for Human Relations in Palos Park, Illinois, noted, "You, as boss, can walk in and put your hand on your secretary's shoulder, but your secretary probably won't walk in and do the same" (Neimark, *Savvy*, 42). It is interesting to note that that comment, published in 1985, does not reflect concerns about sexual touching that have surfaced and become prominent since that time.

Studies do show that men touch more than women. One has only to watch athletic events on television or in person to know that athletes touch each other confidently and casually in the sports arena. Women athletes are beginning to express their emotions and support with touch, too.

One other use of touch that is extremely important, especially among equals, such as colleagues in a meeting situation, for example, is when someone is going on too long, being too vehement, or about to get angry. A light touch on the sleeve of their jacket—with or without accompanying words—has a calming effect.

It is well known that shaking hands, a strong use of touch, is a clear statement of equality, and a woman should certainly recognize that fact, offering her hand in all situations in which she is meeting new people. It is important not to wait, as in the distant past, for the man to extend his hand first. You demonstrate you are putting yourself on the same level or on the same footing with that person when you offer your hand. Women can also take a note from men who routinely shake hands with colleagues and friends from whom they have been absent for as little as two days. Bonding is reinforced.

By the way, be sure your handshake is a firm handshake. Have the appropriate kind of handshake, neither limp nor bone-crushing, by making certain that your approach is correct: palms should lightly touch and the crotches of your thumbs should meet when shaking hands. That eliminates the possibility of your offering a limp, fingers only, handshake. It also minimizes the possibilities of someone crunching your fingers or giving you a limp handshake, consciously or otherwise. However, to insure a full handshake, try this: when you extend your hand, don't extend it with thumb on top; if the palm is slightly upturned, and your hand is at a 45-degree angle (it appears almost able to accept an object) it is virtually impossible to grasp just your fingers.

Acting equal usually means being more assertive. Does being assertive label a woman as "masculine"? Successful women in my profession, in my circle of friends, in my consulting practice, and in my audiences all say a resounding "No!" One woman gleefully raised her hand during a recent speech to reinforce her "No" by relating an experience. She indicated that she had needed a new computer for some time. She had tried all the usual approaches: a memo, a request for equipment, hints. Finally, in desperation, she marched into her supervisor's office, looked her right in the eye, and exclaimed, "I *need* a new computer *now!*" Her supervisor's reaction? "You got it." As she mused about why this tactic had worked when all others had failed—beyond the obvious assertiveness—my comment was, "You finally got her attention." What I meant was that though the computer was of the utmost importance to her, it was only one of many details awaiting her supervisor's attention.

Should people march into their supervisor's office demanding everything they want? Of course not. You must pick your spots. Remember we are talking about a special communications situation. When you need to get someone's specific attention for a specific item or request, be assertive.

Acting equal provides the right degree of assertiveness to help you sound equal.

CHAPTER EIGHT

Sound Like an Equal

> ### In a hurry?
>
> • *put your idea first*
> • *sound assertive*

Once you feel equal and act equal, you begin to recognize that you *can* be listened to. Notice your increased enthusiasm for becoming more powerful? Sounding equal has to do with speaking powerfully and having a good voice.

Get the Attention You Need

You can get people's attention in a variety of ways. Consider use of their name, a touch, a hook, and a pause. In a one-to-one situation, calling a person's name is the best way to get his attention. We like our names (well, anyway, most of us do). We respond to our names. Notice how easy it is to distinguish your name from the babble of unintelligible voices over the loudspeaker at the airport? And isn't it just as easy to pick your name out of an entire page of printed names, in the list of contributors in a program, too?

My favorite example of successful use of a person's name comes from my own dining room. Picture my husband and me seated at the table reading the Sunday paper. Reading the garden section, I find an article about roses that he is not apt to read, but which might be helpful in our rose care. I used to just start reading out loud or talking about it. As I looked up, expectantly waiting for a comment, I could see that his face was still buried deeply in the business section. I felt unhappy he was not giving me the attention I thought I deserved.

But I was wrong to think that, and perhaps wrong to feel unhappy. Why? In fact, I had not gained his attention. I know he is a concentrated reader. He has the ability to block out everything except what he is doing at the moment. So, to communicate with him, I must first get his attention.

The strategy I now use is to lower my own paper and say in a fairly firm voice, "Kent." (That's his name, Kent.) Then I wait. If after fifteen or twenty seconds he has not looked up, I repeat, "Kent," a little louder, a little firmer. I wait again. Usually, between five and twenty seconds later the sound of his name will have penetrated his consciousness. He looks up, tips his paper down, looks toward me, smiles, and says, "Yes?" Having thus gained his attention, I share my article with him. It works nearly every time.

When you walk through the door to your supervisor's office, that person is probably not looking up expectantly at you, even if you had an appointment. She is just hanging up the phone, busy reading a file, or looking through the day's *Business Journal*. You must get your supervisor's attention before you begin to make your point or ask your question.

Pause in the doorway and say, "Nancy"—and wait. You may walk forward or remain in the doorway, depending on the degree of formality that your supervisor expects. Once she looks up at you with an expectant smile or even an assertive scowl, then, and only then, do you begin to make your point.

Because interruptions are so frequent in a day— phones ringing, people coming in and out of our offices, printers clicking, faxes chirping, typewriters clacking, voices everywhere—it is harder and harder to work. People are learning to concentrate more, to block out, to put in mental earplugs in order to concentrate on their work. The trend to open offices and low dividers multiplies the problems of concentration. Therefore, to get people's attention, you must break their concentration, and on a one-to-one basis the easiest way to get a person's attention is by using his name.

Another possibility to get a person's attention is touch. When walking up to a person, touching him or her very lightly on the arm or shoulder gets the attention that you seek. Seated at the breakfast table, I may reach over to touch my husband's hand or arm to gain his attention. Sometimes that works and sometimes it doesn't: he may think I'm simply making an affectionate gesture. In this case, I must tap him firmly. Touch as an attention-getter works well with children and sometimes even with teenagers. Use touch silently. Speak after you have gained attention.

If you are going in to speak to your supervisor or boss, it is less likely that you will use touch, although, depending upon the relationship, sometimes you can. See Chapter Seven for a fuller discussion of the do's and don't-do's of touching.

Get the Attention of a Small Group

When you begin to say something, especially if you happen to be the first to comment on a topic, other people's minds are usually somewhere else thinking about something else—how hot it is, how much work has been set aside in order to come to the meeting, what to do about a sick spouse. Your need for an attention getter is the need to get their minds on the topic you are about to talk about, the opinion you are about to express.

Milo O. Frank has captured the essence of the attention-getter in his book, *How to Get Your Point Across in Thirty Seconds or Less*. He calls it the "hook." Frank says,

> *A hook is a statement or an object used specifically to get attention. Hooks are dangled*

in front of you every hour of the day and night as you watch television, listen to the radio, read newspapers, books and magazines, and look at billboards. (p. 40.)

He suggests that hooks are whatever it is that entices, tempts, tantalizes, fascinates, attracts, catches, or makes you remember. He points out how clearly we see this in our daily life in terms of advertising, newspaper headlines, teasers for television and radio programs. The hook is your attention-getting device. You, too, must tempt, tantalize, captivate, attract, and catch the attention of your audience.

Usually that hook involves content directly related to what you are about to say. It can be a question, provided the question is short, strongly phrased and strongly expressed—verbally and non-verbally. Other possibilities for attention getters or openers include statistics, dramatic or vital statements, and brief descriptive openers that will help the listeners get tuned in to what you are going to say. You may use some of the same devices for your attention getter in a committee situation that you would use in a speech. In *Speaking To a Group* (see Chapter Three), the section on developing the opener includes many ideas for hooks.

Pauses are also useful as attention getters. If you make part of a statement and pause just before the key point, people tend to lean forward to hear what will follow the pause. They are intrigued to hear what you're going to say next, how you are going to finish the sentence. An example: "Our strategy to invite involvement [pause] a contest!" This type of pause creates suspense. A pause works the same way when you are using a person's name. I say, "Kent," and I pause, waiting for him to peer over the newspaper. When you walk to the door of your boss's office, you say, "Nancy," then pause until she looks up.

Make One Point, Up Front

Once you have the attention you need and you open your mouth to begin speaking (or you follow the hook with the second sentence), put your idea, opinion, or observation, in the very next sentence. If you wish to be listened to, do not play games, be indirect, or beat around the bush. Put your point there. Make it clear and concise. Support it with one sentence or one idea, and then stop. Stopping is not the hardest part; you just have to close your mouth!

Assume you have been given authority and responsibility for the annual sales meeting. You are sitting in a meeting and the chair says, "Marsha, how's the sales meeting coming along?" (That chairperson would have better directed you by saying, "Give us a brief update about the sales meeting," because that is the way facilitators of meetings encourage people to be brief, but your facilitator did not do that.)

Unless you're careful, what you say when you open your mouth might go something like this:

> *Well, it's going to be good. You know, we took a poll of the employees and they all said they wanted to go to the Coast, and Salishan*

was the number one choice, but Salishan just turned out to be too expensive for us, and so we looked around and just couldn't find, on the weekend that we were looking for, what else we wanted. So it's going to be at the Inn of the Seventh Mountain, and that's okay because everybody likes it in the mountains, too. I've had some trouble with the registration process because my assistant's wife was transferred, so he had to quit, but everything's coming along fine and...

Here, at long last, is the point: "Everything's coming along fine." Does that sound painfully familiar? What should you have said?

"Everything's arranged. It's at the Inn of the Seventh Mountain, April 29th through 30th. Details will be handed out after the meeting. If you want it point by point, I'll be happy to give it to you."

Two guesses on how many times they want you to go over it all point by point, and the first guess does not count. Virtually zero percent of the time will a group want to hear all the details.

Recognize what you are also doing here at the meeting level is the same thing you do at the conversational level. Give your main point first. If you want discussion, build it by giving a little bit and having someone ask a question, giving a little bit more and having someone add a comment. It is done in the same way that building a dialogue is important in answering questions (see Chapter Three).

An at-home example goes something like this: Your spouse says, "Shall we go to the movies tonight?" Your up-front response would be, "Yes, that sounds wonderful." Or, "No, I'm kind of tired; let's just rent a movie." If you're like me, what you tend to say instead is,

> *Oh, gee, we haven't been out in a long time, that would be fun, but you know, the last time we went to the movies on Saturday night, we decided we were never going to go again because it was such a hassle and we couldn't find a place to park. Remember? The kids in the theater were so noisy and it was so dirty. Maybe we ought to just rent a movie instead. What do you think?*

Let me summarize the problems from that example: Women tend to talk in paragraphs. Women tend to give too many details. People who have subordinate behavior tend to not be able to express an opinion. People who have subordinate behavior tend to close on a question rather than on a statement. Powerful people tend to tell, and subordinate or unpowerful people tend to ask. Case closed.

Have Strong Vocal Qualities

The final aspect of sounding like an equal is having a good voice. Your voice is a key instrument in developing yourself as a powerful person and certainly a key instrument in getting people to pay attention when you talk. If you believe what you are saying, that belief will be reflected in your voice. Your listener will hear it.

Consider four vocal features:

- volume
- rate
- quality
- tone.

Volume

When analyzing your voice, pay attention to its volume. Many women are afraid to speak loudly because they have been told a loud voice sounds too masculine. What you are concerned about, of course, is being heard. It is certainly possible for women to speak loudly and still be considered women. As a friend of mine suggests, "It is better to be heard than to be disregarded." If you have doubt, ask your friends or colleagues about your volume.

Rate

Your rate of speed reflects your emotional state more than any other vocal aspect. If you speak too slowly, you appear to be uncertain. If you speak too fast, you appear to be angry, nervous, or uncertain whether people will listen to you. A measured pause reflects confidence.

How many of you have developed the habit of speaking rapidly so that you can get what you wish to say out before you get interrupted? As a child, I was a stutterer. I am convinced that the problem developed because I played with older boys (not having any girls my age around), and they did interrupt me—not only because I was younger, but also because I was a girl. I tried to get what I wanted to say out quickly, couldn't always get it out quickly, and stuttered. After learning to slow down and to speak more forcefully, they quit interrupting, and I quit stuttering.

Quality

Quality is a difficult feature to pin down because it changes so much. The culprit is whining. Some people tend to whine when they are feeling put upon or helpless. Whining can become such a bad habit that you have a whining tone even though there's nothing to whine about. Monitor this aspect carefully. Ask your spouse, a friend, or older child to tell you honestly if (and when) you have a whining tone in your voice. Nothing turns a male audience off any quicker than a whining voice. Females are a bit more tolerant, but women do each other a disservice to be so. Whining is also a problem for older people.

If you have serious voice problems—an extremely high-pitched voice, for example—you may wish to see a professional voice coach. But most people have a perfectly adequate, pleasant voice if they learn to use it well. You can profitably use an audiotape of your voice to listen to quality and distracting voice mannerisms—such as "uh," "and uh," "you know," "like," or "he goes" (a misuse of the verb "he said," which has become endemic to the entire younger population of the country).

Tone

The tones used to create good verbal sound are similar to the tones used to create good singing. While you do not need to be a singer to have good vocal quality, you can learn their techniques to improve your voice. One technique comes from Dr. Morton Cooper, who wrote a book called *Change Your Voice, Change Your Life*. It contains a simple exercise you can practice to develop good vocal color. Dr. Cooper indicates that most voices have more than one pitch level—a routine or habitual level and a natural level. He says that many people tend to use a pitch that is too low. That is, their routine or habitual level is not their appropriate pitch. The natural pitch is the one that allows you to control the sounds you make.

Here's Dr. Cooper's simple technique:

> *Say* umm-hmmm *using rising inflection with the lips closed. It is vital that this* umm-hmmm *be spontaneous and sincere. The sound you are producing should be your right voice. This is your natural pitch enhanced by tone focus. If you are doing exactly what I asked of you, you will feel a slight tingling or vibration around the nose and lips. This indicates correct tone focus with oral nasal resonance. If your pitch is too low, which occurs in most cases of voice misuse, you will feel too much vibration in the lower throat and very little if any at all in the mask area. Repeat the exercise, saying* umm-hmmm *to determine if you are doing it properly. Make a correction if necessary until*

*you feel the tingling sensation about the lips
and nose .... This is the voice you will learn to
use all the time.... This should be your natural
voice, your right voice.* (p. 23, 26.)

Try this simple technique. Once you have found
that spot and learned to speak in that tone, you will
be pleased and excited about the vocal variety you
can get into your words. You can make your voice
sound firm enough to be heard across a room. You
can make your voice sound strong enough to be powerful.

Once you have found the right spot with *umm-
hmmm*, use the word *hello* to practice vocal variety
and strength. If you can say the word *hello* using three
or four different levels of pitch—He-*LL-ll*-oo—you
will know you have found the right spot. Call me at
503-293-1163 for over-the-phone help! As you continue to improve your vocal variety, you will be more
confident. You will feel stronger about this part of
your communications skills. You can sound powerful.

CHAPTER NINE

Look Like an Equal

In a hurry?

- *dress to meet the level of the decision-maker*

An old saying goes "you never get a second chance to make a first impression." It is true that people who know you already have an impression of you; however, you can modify that impression, gradually. When you meet new people, you start with a new impression. When you approach situations in which you wish to be powerful, you have an opportunity to make a fresh first impression by looking equal to the people you are speaking to. Consider these four aspects of looking equal:

- meet the level of your audience
- earn respect

- adopt a conservative approach
- let appearance enhance confidence.

Meet the Level of Your Audience

The basic rule of appearance is to dress to meet the level of your audience, even if it is a one-to-one encounter. If the group is varied, dress to the level of the highest-ranking person. Assume you are addressing a meeting or giving a committee report. Even though there are people present from different strata of the organization, your appearance should be equal to that of the highest ranking person there. Please note, especially for women, this does not mean looking "the same as." This means looking "equal to."

When your audience is male management, you do not necessarily have to wear the same grey pin-stripe suit with white shirt and little bow tie, John Molloy's *Dress For Success* notwithstanding. There are professions and situations where that same appearance may be appropriate, but more on that later. The first concern is to look equal to your audience. People do business most comfortably with people like themselves. And this statement is just as true for men as it is for women.

Imagine a middle manager who has been asked to make a report to the board of directors. As this manager walks into the room prior to the meeting, he discovers that all the male board members are dressed in grey or navy suits, the women dressed in equally elegant or expensive suits. This middle manager looks down to note he is wearing a brown tweed jacket, brown slacks, argyle socks, and brown shoes. He realizes instantly, as do you, that he is at a distinct disadvantage. Why? Because he looks different from the rest of the people in the room.

He looks different, and he also looks less powerful. Grey and navy are considered power colors for men; brown is not. His non-verbal appearance message is "I am less powerful." Can he still be successful in making his report and gaining their confidence? He can. But by appearing different, he puts a huge barrier between him and his audience that will make it more difficult for him to be successful. The moment these board members see him is the moment they begin to think, "Unh-unh, going to vote no." It is often not even a conscious thought. It is a reaction to the non-verbal message that his appearance sends. They will be voting against his appearance, not his proposal.

You may remember a cartoon in the *Harvard Business Review* that depicted a staffer approaching the desk of the boss, wearing a polka dot bow tie. Over the head of the boss was the international *no* symbol, a circle with a slash, imposed upon a polka dot bow tie. That poor young man didn't even get to open his mouth before his idea was rejected, because he did not look equal.

The same is true for a woman. Assume you are a secretary going in to ask your supervisor for a promotion to administrative assistant. If you wear a blouse and flowered skirt, with dangling earrings and bangle bracelets, your image is not that of an equal. Your non-verbal message shouts "support staff," or "not yet professional." Prepare for that meeting by observing carefully the appearance of your boss. You have two options: 1) dress, insofar as you are able, as she does, or 2) dress appropriately for the position or responsibility that you are asking for.

Sometimes it is a balancing act. I recall a conversation with a client who wanted to clarify an aspect of appearance. She began with stories about her success as a national trainer. Her area of expertise is support staff communications. She indicated her best success with these groups of secretaries and support staff comes when she wears a suit composed of a quilted, flowered jacket and a solid, slim skirt. When she wears more conservative, professional looking suits, the response of her audience is not as good. Her quilted jacket with unmatched skirt, while still professional, made her appear more like her audience. Because they can identify with her appearance, they are more apt to be accepting of her message.

She does look more expensively dressed than they do, which is appropriate, even necessary, for an outside speaker. In addition, she should dress to the top of the group, and the boss may be present. This is where the balancing act comes in. The boss will expect this speaker to be her equal. The support staff will expect her to look like a professional speaker—an expert—who is getting paid substantial money to do training. Her solution, an expensive suit with a separates look, allows her to balance these requirements comfortably.

Earn Respect

Consider the experience of a woman whose husband was president of a national consultant's organization. She was a bit of a rebel and not interested in, as she said, "playing clothing games." When she accompanied her husband to regional and national conferences she typically wore good-looking velour workout clothes or casual but expensive pants and sweaters. Occasionally, she chose a casual skirt outfit. The rest of us, both consultants and spouses, tended to dress in our professional best. As she and I went to breakfast one morning, she confessed great frustration because a variety of people treated her in ways she considered inappropriate: giving her the briefest greeting, ignoring her altogether, or patronizing her. She felt she deserved more respect, both as an individual and as the wife of the president of the organization.

I tactfully conveyed to her that her appearance was sending the wrong message. She was non-verbally communicating the message, "I'm not very important. Don't pay much attention to me. Don't treat me like an equal because I don't think of myself as an equal." Not being a psychologist, I could not assess with her why she chose to send this mixed message. But our conversation enabled her to see that she had options. She could dress more professionally, sending an "I'm equal" message. Or, if she wished to continue to send this message by her appearance, she should be prepared for the consequences of that message.

Adopt a Conservative Approach

The approach suggested here in looking like an equal is admittedly a conservative one. Women pride themselves on individuality; they would like to have it both ways—to be fully accepted into the business community and to dress as individuals, not as male clones. Sometimes this approach is possible; other times they have to make at least an initial choice: individuality or success.

When you want people to pay attention and take you seriously, some compromise to an all-out individualist stance is often necessary. As mentioned earlier, the game has been going on for a long time and when you come to bat, if you wish to make a hit you will be more successful if you pay some attention to the rules of the game. If you choose to ignore the rules, you may still succeed. But you will likely have additional hurdles to overcome, like the man in the brown tweed jacket at the board meeting.

When you overtly or unconsciously dress in a manner other than what your audience expects or is comfortable with, you create an additional problem for the listener. He has to try to understand what message you are sending with your appearance. That understanding may get in the way of hearing your message. Sometimes a person tunes you out based on appearance rather than on the merit of your idea or suggestion.

If you wish to be successful in specific communication situations, you must get people to pay attention to you. Therefore, the bottom line in terms of appearance is, "If in doubt, don't." If the jangling bracelets create a distraction, leave them off. If the oversized earrings are in question, put on some smaller ones. If the choice is between a contrasting blazer or a matching jacket, choose the matching outfit. If you are concerned that your appearance might not look professional enough, enhance it.

It is better to err on the side of conservative than on the side of flamboyant. You know from looking around as you walk down the streets that men tend, in most business professions, to be more conservative than women. Opting for conservatism, when you are looking like an equal, presents you with greater opportunity for success.

In terms of appearance in the long term, once you have become powerful, you can then adopt a more individualistic look. Do it gradually.

Let Appearance Enhance Confidence

Yet another reason to dress professionally, particularly when you wish to get someone's attention, is that you usually feel more confident when you are more dressed up. If you are casual in dress, you tend to be casual in mentality. As people add the costume—the outward accoutrements of professionalism—nearly everyone tends to behave in a more professional way. And if any message is coming through in this book, it is that being appropriately professional to a given situation is important if you want people in business to listen to you.

How does appearance affect your ability to communicate at home with your spouse or significant other? Darned if I know. But I surmise that it does make some difference. My spouse is around professional looking people (including women) all day, and my instincts tell me that if I am slopping around in a ragged old housecoat, I am less apt to look like a person he needs to pay much attention to. Let me know what you come up with.

In terms of appearance, perhaps the key is that you do have choices. As long as you know what your appearance is saying, what non-verbal message you are sending, you may ignore the suggestions and still be successful. If you lean to flamboyant or frivolous, feminine, artistic, sloppy or casual, and do not get the attentive results you desire, consider a change in your appearance.

A Final Note

Getting others to listen is not simply a matter of fight or switch. Insofar as age is a factor, both parents of all ages and children of all ages must try harder to be respectful and courteous, even if it means listening to things they would just as soon tune out. Insofar as gender is a factor, both men and women must continue to work to open lines of communicating, especially in one-to-one communicating. In the business and professional world, a continued awareness of strengths and weaknesses of the communications styles of both men and women will enhance harmony in the work place and profits at the bottom line.

Your bottom line is this: if something isn't working, fix it. Make changes that will enhance your effectiveness and increase your power by improving your ability to get others to listen.

Additional Resources

Cooper, Dr. Morton. *Change Your Voice, Change Your Life*. New York: Perennial Library, Harper & Row, Publishers, 1985.

Fishman, Pamela M. Revised version in *Language, Gender and Society*, ed. by Barrie Thorne, Cheris Kramarae, and Nancy Henley, 89-101. Rowley, MA: Newbury House, 1983.

Frank, Milo. *How to Get Your Point Across in 30 Seconds or Less*. New York: Simon & Schuster, Inc., 1986.

Lakoff, Robin. *Language and Women's Place*. New York: Harper and Row, 1975.

LeRoux, Paul. *Selling to a Group*. New York: Harper & Row, Publishers, Barnes & Noble Books, 1984.

Neimark, Jill. "Reach Out and ..." *Savvy*, New York, February, 1985.

Tannen, Deborah. *You Just Don't Understand: Women and Men in Conversation*. New York: William Morrow and Company, 1990.

Woodall, Marian K. *Speaking to a Group—Mastering the SKILL of Public Speaking*. Lake Oswego, OR: Professional Business Communications, 1990.

Woodall, Marian K. *Thinking on Your Feet—Answering Questions Well, Whether You Know the Answer or NOT!* Lake Oswego, OR: Professional Business Communications, 1987.

Zimmerman, Don H., and Candace West. "Sex Roles, Interruptions and Silences in Conversation." *Language and Sex: Difference and Dominance,* ed. by Barrie Thorne and Nancy Henley, 105-129. Rowley, MA: Newbury House, 1975.

Marian K. Woodall is the author of *Thinking on Your Feet*, *Speaking to a Group*, and *How to Talk So Men Will Listen*. She is available to speak or to present seminars on these topics and a wide range of other oral communications topics. Her professionalism, enthusiasm, and lively style will highlight your meeting or conference.

Additional copies of the books, *How to Talk So Men Will Listen* ($7.95), *Speaking to a Group* ($15.95), *Thinking on Your Feet* ($9.95), and a two-cassette (two hours) audiotape companion program to *Thinking on Your Feet* ($19.95) are available. Please add a shipping charge of $1.55 to the total cost of your order. VISA and Mastercard welcome.

Call: 800/447-5911 for orders.
      503/293-1163 for inquiries.

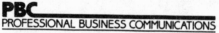

PBC
PROFESSIONAL BUSINESS COMMUNICATIONS
11830 S.W. Kerr Parkway, Suite 350
Lake Oswego, Oregon 97035

Please send copies of the following:

THINKING ON YOUR FEET

_____ book(s) @ $9.95 each

_____ audio tape package(s) @ $19.95 each

SPEAKING TO A GROUP

_____ book(s) @ $15.95 each

HOW TO TALK SO MEN WILL LISTEN

_____ book(s) @ $7.95 each

_____
Name

_____
Addresss

_____
City   /   State /   Zip Code

Please send copies of the following:

THINKING ON YOUR FEET

_____ book(s) @ $9.95 each

_____ audio tape package(s) @ $19.95 each

SPEAKING TO A GROUP

_____ book(s) @ $15.95 each

HOW TO TALK SO MEN WILL LISTEN

_____ book(s) @ $7.95 each

_____
Name

_____
Addresss

_____
City   /   State /   Zip Code